THE LIFESKILLS LIBRARY

Staying Healthy

Jane Hurwitz
Sue Hurwitz

THE ROSEN PUBLISHING GROUP, INC.

NEW YORK

Published in 1993 by The Rosen Publishing Group, Inc.
29 East 21st Street, New York, NY 10010

First Edition
Copyright 1993 by The Rosen Publishing Group, Inc.

Manufactured in the United States of America.

Library of Congress Cataloging-in-Publication Data

Hurwitz, Jane.
    Staying healthy / Jane Hurwitz, Sue Hurwitz.
       p.   cm. — (The Life skills library)
    Includes bibliographical references and index.
    Summary: Presents information for teenagers on diet, nutrition, vitamins, exercise, visiting the doctor, safer sex, birth control, and personal hygiene.
    ISBN 0-8239-1471-2
    1. Teenagers—Health and hygiene—Juvenile literature.
[1. Health. 2. Grooming. 3. Life skills.]   I. Hurwitz, Sue, 1934-.
II. Title III. Series.
RA777.H85 1993
613'.0433--dc20   92-42125
                                       CIP
                                       AC

CONTENTS

INTRODUCTION

Every day you make choices about your health and physical fitness. Will you eat breakfast or skip it? Will you brush your teeth or not? Will you eat healthful foods or "junk foods"? Will you exercise or just sit around and watch TV?

Doctors know that a great many teenagers are overweight. They know that teenagers eat foods with too much fat, sugar, and salt. They know that teenagers exercise too little. That puts teenagers at risk for heart disease, high blood pressure, and high cholesterol levels.

As a teenager, your body changes rapidly. Yet not all teenagers mature at the same rate. Everyone requires different amounts of food and fitness. Those needs change as your body changes.

Still, there are certain healthful habits that we should all try to incorporate into our daily lives. This book is about building a healthy mind and a healthy body. It tells you what doctors think are healthful choices for food and fitness. It tells you what doctors think will help prevent illness. It tells you where you can go for help.

It is simply not enough to read how to make good choices about food and physical fitness. You must do something with what you learn. You must not only get fit, but you must stay fit.

It is your responsibility to take good care of yourself. No one else can do it for you. You have the power to keep your body working at its best. You have the power to change the way you look and feel.

Healthful habits do not just develop overnight. They must be learned and continued every day. You only have one body. The choices you make now will affect your health as an adult. You are in control of taking care of yourself. Staying healthy and fit is something you do for yourself. And you can enjoy doing it!

FOOD FOR A
HEALTHY BODY
AND MIND

You may have heard the saying, "You are what you eat." In some ways that is true. What you eat and drink make up your "diet." Diet plays a big part in how you look and feel. A healthful diet helps your body work at its best. It also helps to prevent or to shorten many illnesses.

Nutrients are the parts of foods that help your body grow and repair itself. There are 50 known nutrients, divided into 5 groups, plus water. The groups are: proteins, carbohydrates, fats, minerals, and vitamins.

Most foods contain several kinds of nutrients. Still, you should choose foods from each food group every day to be sure that you get many of the nutrients that your body needs.

—

A well-balanced diet and regular exercise are important for staying healthy.

Proteins

Proteins are nutrients used by the body for growth, repair, and energy. Proteins build bone and muscle. Your brain, hair, and skin are made up of proteins. Proteins are part of the red blood cells that carry oxygen around your body. Proteins also build antibodies in your blood. Antibodies help protect you from diseases.

Proteins contain 20 nutrients that the body needs. These are called *amino acids.* The amino acids work together to make thousands of different proteins. Your body can make nearly all the amino acids it needs. But there are eight that your body cannot make. You must eat these in foods.

Foods that contain all eight amino acids are called complete proteins. Meat, fish, chicken, eggs, and milk are examples of complete proteins.

Incomplete proteins are foods that have some, but not all eight, amino acids. Several incomplete proteins may be eaten together or with dairy foods to get complete proteins. Beans, dried peas, nuts, seeds, breads, grains, and cereals are all examples of incomplete proteins.

Vegetarian Diets

People who do not eat foods made from animals are called *vegetarians.* Vegetarians mix incomplete proteins to get a composite of the same nutrients found in complete proteins. Brown rice, grains, and whole wheat bread are examples of vegetarian foods. So are spaghetti, macaroni, noodles, fresh fruits, and fresh vegetables. Some vegetarians also eat milk and eggs.

Many doctors think it is healthier to eat less meat than most Americans do today. They say that eating meat and eggs three times a week is often enough. Eating whole grains, fresh fruits, and vegetables adds fiber (bulk) to the diet.

Fiber is a part of food that is not digested by the body. It is important to include fiber in your diet. Fiber speeds food through the digestive system. This helps prevent constipation. Some doctors say that a high-fiber diet may help to prevent bowel cancer. Fiber also gives you a feeling of fullness. That helps keep you from feeling hungry.

Carbohydrates

Carbohydrates provide quick energy. Sugar and starch are carbohydrates. Starch is found in bread, noodles, potatoes, and rice. Starch is also found in most yellow or white vegetables. Nonstarchy vegetables are usually green and leafy.

Natural sugar is found in fresh fruits such as grapefruit, oranges, peaches, and plums. Sugar is also found in some vegetables and in milk. Sugar has many names. Dextrose, lactose, maltose, and sucrose are some that you may not know. Other sugars are corn syrup, maple syrup, molasses, and honey. Many processed (man-made) foods such as ketchup, mayonnaise, crackers, soups, and salad dressings contain sugar.

Processed sugar (sugar that is added to foods) is not a good choice for a healthful diet . Too much sugar may cause tooth decay and weight gain. It may, along with obesity, aggravate diabetes. Diabetes is a disease that people get when their bodies cannot process sugar normally.

For good health, you should eat as little processed sugar as possible. Candy, sugared cereals, sweet rolls, cake, pie, ice cream, chocolate, and cola drinks are foods that have large amounts of processed sugar.

Foods with high amounts of processed sugar and fats are called "junk food." Junk food usually does not have a good balance of nutrients. If you need a snack between meals it is better to choose fruit, cheese, carrots, nuts, or seeds.

Many foods and drinks contain artificial sweeteners such as saccharin or aspartame (NutraSweet). They are sold as "diet" foods. Some doctors say that large amounts of artificial sweeteners may cause headaches or cancer.

Fats and Cholesterol

Fats are nutrients that give you energy. Fats also help your body store energy and vitamins.

Cholesterol is a substance that helps to carry important fatty acids through your bloodstream. Your liver makes most of the cholesterol your body needs. The rest comes from food. High levels of cholesterol in the blood have been shown to contribute to heart disease.

There are three kinds of fat: saturated, unsaturated, and polyunsaturated. Usually, saturated fats are solid at room temperature; unsaturated fats are liquid. Saturated fats tend to raise the cholesterol in the blood.

There are two classifications of unsaturated fats. They are known as monounsaturated or polyunsaturated fats. Monounsaturated fats tend to increase the "good" cholesterol, called HDL for short. Polyunsaturated fats tend to reduce the total level of cholesterol, reducing the "good" HDL as well.

Foods containing unsaturated fats include fish, grains, fruits, and vegetables.

Foods containing saturated fats include ice cream, whole milk, meat, butter, margarine, and most fried foods.

Egg yolk (the yellow part), liver, and cheese are foods that are high in cholesterol.

Minerals

Minerals are nutrients that build and strengthen bones and teeth. Minerals keep the body's red blood cells and digestive juices healthy. Only very small amounts of minerals are needed by the body. Calcium, iron, sodium, fluoride, and zinc are important minerals.

Calcium helps build strong bones and teeth and helps control your heartbeat. Calcium also helps your blood to clot and your muscles to relax. Calcium is found in milk, yogurt, cheese, sardines, peanuts, and dark green leafy vegetables.

Doctors agree that drinking three 8-ounce glasses of low-fat or skim milk every day is good for teen-agers. Whole milk (which contains 4 percent fat) is not as good a choice. If you are allergic to milk, unsweetened low-fat yogurt often can replace it in your diet.

Iron helps the blood carry oxygen in your blood-stream. If your body doesn't get enough iron, you may feel tired. Iron is found in dried beans, peas, clams, egg yolks, liver, meat, poultry, fish, spinach, and prunes.

Sodium, or salt, is found naturally in many foods. Salt is also added to instant foods, canned foods, and pickled foods. Luncheon meats and most snacks have added salt as well. Doctors say that adding too much salt to your food may lead to high blood pressure and strokes.

Fluoride helps protect your teeth from decay. A small amount of fluoride is found naturally in water or added to the water supply. Fluoride is used by many dentists when they clean your teeth.

Zinc helps your taste buds develop and work normally. Zinc is found in fruits, vegetables, milk products, and whole-grain bread and cereals.

—

Nutritious meals can be prepared with fresh foods and wholesome ingredients.

Vitamins

Vitamins are nutrients that help your body use proteins, carbohydrates, and fats. Vitamins help protect you from infections. Only small amounts of vitamins are needed to build and keep a healthy body.

Our bodies need many different vitamins. There are two major types of vitamins. Vitamins A, D, E, and K are stored in body fat. They do not need to be replaced every day. Taking large amounts of these vitamins in pills can be harmful.

Vitamins B and C cannot be stored by the body. They must be replaced through your daily diet.

Vitamin C is needed in order for your body to heal properly. It keeps your teeth and gums healthy and helps your body use iron. Vitamin C helps to maintain the proper condition of your blood vessels and helps your body fight diseases. Your body cannot make Vitamin C. Foods containing Vitamin C should be eaten every day.

Oranges and orange juice, grapefruit, lemons, limes, strawberries, tomatoes, potatoes, broccoli, cabbage, cauliflower, and spinach are good sources of Vitamin C.

The B vitamins are a group of nutrients that keep your skin, eyes, and nerves healthy. You should eat foods with B vitamins every day.

Niacin, thiamine, and riboflavin are three of the B vitamins. They are found in whole-grain cereals and enriched or whole-wheat breads. They are also found in brown rice, nuts, tuna, chicken, meat, liver, pork, eggs, and mushrooms. Riboflavin is found in milk, yogurt, cottage cheese, and green leafy vegetables.

Vitamins may be eaten in pills. But vitamin pills do not take the place of a healthful diet. You can get all the vitamins you need by eating plenty of fruits and vegetables every day.

Water

Water is the body's most important nutrient. You could live for months on the nutrients stored in your body. But you could live only about three days without water.

Water carries nutrients to all parts of the body. Your blood is mostly water. Water keeps your body temperature normal. Water also flushes wastes out of the body.

You should drink at least four 8-ounce glasses of water every day. Water is much better for you than soft drinks that contain caffeine or sugar.

Your goal should be to eat a wide variety of foods. A healthful diet includes protein, carbohydrates, fruits, vegetables, milk products, and plenty of water. It should be low in fat, saturated fat and cholesterol, sugar, and salt.

You should take care not to overeat and become overweight. But you should not fast or starve yourself on a "crash diet," either. You should never skip meals when you are watching your weight. Your body needs nutrients to stay healthy. People who do not get enough of the right foods often suffer from malnutrition.

Remember, your body was not built in one day. You cannot change it in one day either. Learning healthful food choices is a long-term goal. You must make good food choices one meal at a time.

Health and Your Mind

The connection between your mind and your body is very complicated. But it is known that your mind and body act together. The brain is responsible for your thinking, decision-making, memory, imagination, and emotions. Your moods and feelings, or emotions, play a big part in keeping you healthy.

Your diet affects your brain as well as your body. Protein foods are important for brain growth. Oxygen is also vital. Your heart pumps oxygen-rich blood to your brain. Without oxygen your brain cells would die in about five minutes. Once brain cells die, your body cannot replace them.

Your emotions play a big part in the foods you choose to eat. When you are in a hurry, you choose different foods than when you sit down to a holiday meal. When you feel good, you choose different foods than when you are sick.

Your self-image, or the way you feel about yourself, affects your health. When you have a positive self-image you feel good about yourself. You are more likely to make good food choices.

When you have a negative self-image you do not feel good about yourself. You may not be thinking clearly. You may be tempted to make poor food choices as well as other bad choices, like using drugs, alcohol, or tobacco. Any mind-altering drugs will not solve problems. They just create more problems!

Mental exercise is important to your health. You need to give yourself time to think and to dream. Thinking keeps your mind active. Reading and learning new ideas help you cope with stress. When your mind gets overloaded you need to relax.

Learning how to relax mentally will help you feel better about yourself and your life. Deep-breathing exercises, physical exercise, reading, and listening to music are all good ways to relax.

Listen to your mind and your body. When you feel stressed, exercising your mind will help relax your body. And exercising your body will help relax your mind. Remember, your mind and your body work together to make you who you are.

HEALTH
AND PHYSICAL
FITNESS

Being physically fit means that your body is as healthy as possible. You stay physically fit by eating healthful foods and by exercising.

Exercise helps to develop your body and to build strong muscles and bones. Exercise also helps your body to build endurance. Endurance is the ability to keep moving for long periods of time. Plenty of exercise also helps you sleep well and decreases fatigue. Exercise helps you control your weight and your outward appearance.

Regular exercise helps your heartbeat become stronger. It gives you more energy. Exercise is good for the mind, too. It helps you deal with the stresses in your life.

—

A daily routine of exercise increases energy levels and produces a sense of well-being.

Endurance Exercise

Endurance exercise helps your heart to beat faster and your body to build good blood vessels. Your breathing rate becomes quicker and deeper. Endurance exercise can also help you lose weight.

Exercises that build heart and lung endurance are called *aerobic* exercises. The word aerobic comes from the Greek word meaning "with oxygen." Aerobic exercises use the body's large muscles for long periods of time. That makes your body need to use more oxygen.

Walking fast, running, biking, dancing, skiing, swimming, skating, and jumping rope are all good forms of aerobic exercise. You should do some kind of regular aerobic exercise for about 30 minutes at least 3 times a week.

Muscle Strength

Poor muscle fitness can lead to low-back pain and poor posture. Exercises that develop muscle strength are usually done for shorter periods of time than aerobic exercises. You should do this kind of exercise for about 20 minutes twice a week.

Exercises with free weights and weight machines help build muscular strength and endurance. Muscular endurance means that your muscles are strong enough to work for long periods of time. Sit-ups, push-ups, and pull-ups help build muscle strength and endurance.

Flexibility

Flexibility is the amount of movement your bones can make at your joints. Stretching, reaching, and bending exercises develop flexibility. These warm-ups help prevent sports-related injuries. The best times to do stretching exercises are just before and after aerobic exercise.

Walking, swimming, skating, and skiing develop flexibility. So do basketball, soccer, softball, and bowling.

Calories

Calories measure the energy that your body gets from food. When your body uses up energy, that is also measured in calories. A pound of body fat equals 3,500 calories. Physical activity burns up calories. You must exercise enough to burn up 3,500 calories for every 3,500 calories of food that you eat. Otherwise, your body will store the extra calories as body fat.

Physical exercise is important. But it also is important to give your body a rest. Your body rests during sleep. Your heart beats more slowly. You take fewer breaths. That gives your lungs a rest.

Check with your doctor before you begin a diet or physical exercise program.

Germs (bacteria and viruses) are in the air all around us. Germs get on our skin. Soap and water wash away dirt and sweat. Soap and water also wash away germs. You should wash your hands whenever they are dirty. But there are special times when washing your hands helps keep you healthy.

Washing your hands before you eat keeps germs from getting into your food. You also should wash your hands before preparing foods or handling dishes or silverware.

Always wash your hands with soap and water after using the bathroom. Washing your hands before going to sleep is also important. When you sleep you often rub your eyes or mouth. If your hands are dirty, germs can enter your body that way.

Doctors believe that oily skin is a major cause of acne (pimples). Washing your face and neck every morning and night helps keep your skin from getting too oily.

Bad Choices

Eating junk food and snacking between meals are unhealthy choices. They lead to weight problems and tooth decay. Through X-rays, dentists can find small cavities in your teeth. Filling cavities while they are small may prevent further decay.

Many kinds of sodas contain caffeine and sugar. Coffee, tea, and chocolate also contain caffeine. Too much caffeine is not good for you and should be limited in your diet.

Drugs, alcohol, and tobacco are unhealthy choices. Most teens know the huge risks of using them. And most teens learn how to deal with peer pressure that encourages their use.

Yet many teenagers give in to peer pressure to have sex. They do not understand the risks of unprotected sex. Many diseases are passed from one partner to the other during sexual activity. But HIV (human immunodeficiency virus), which causes AIDS (acquired immunodeficiency syndrome), is the most dangerous sexually transmitted disease.

AIDS kills! Doctors do not yet have a cure for AIDS or HIV. AIDS attacks the body's white blood cells. A person infected with AIDS cannot fight off infections or allergies.

The AIDS virus is carried in blood and other body fluids. AIDS can be spread by sharing needles during drug use or by sexual activity.

Using condoms (male protection) during sexual activity is thought to be safe. That is misleading. Condoms provide *safer* sex than using no protection at all. But condoms are *not* 100 percent safe.

There is only one way to be 100 percent safe from sexual disease. That is to say "no" to sex.

You make important decisions every day about your health, your body, and your life. You should think carefully about the decision to have sex. Choosing safer sex is a smart decision. Choosing no sex is a decision that may save your life!

EATING DISORDERS

Lorna was 14 and overweight. Meals were important family gatherings in her home. Her mom spent most of the day in the kitchen. Lorna's whole family had weight problems.

"I am so fat that I will never get a date," Lorna complained to her friend Haley, who was also overweight. "I hate the way I look! I'm going on a crash diet."

Haley sighed. They had both gone on diets so often that she lost count. "You know what Mrs. Bernard said at school. You need to diet *and* exercise to lose weight. Maybe that makes more sense."

"I remember," Lorna said. "Will you try it with me? We can help each other if we stick together."

Some people eat because of loneliness or boredom.

Getting Started

That evening Lorna helped set the table for dinner. During the meal she covered her plate with salad so her parents wouldn't see how little she was eating.

Lorna began skipping breakfast and lunch. She barely ate dinner. And she exercised too much. She became weak, but she thought that thin people normally felt weak.

After several weeks, Lorna began to feel thinner. But Haley went off her diet.

"I just can't give up food!" Haley complained. "I want to be thin, but I just can't diet."

"My parents only see me at dinner. As long as I pretend to eat, they don't notice me," Lorna said. "You are the only one who has even noticed that I've lost weight!"

Lorna lost ten pounds during the next month. She began to look thinner. And so did Haley.

"You look thinner!" Lorna remarked one evening when Haley came over. "Are you dieting again?"

"No, I couldn't," Haley confessed. "I'm forcing myself to vomit right after I eat. I'm also taking laxatives to get rid of any food that is left!"

"Oh, that's not right," Lorna said. "Mrs. Bernard told us that you can develop a disease called *bulimia* from that!"

"I'm not bulimic!" Haley insisted. "I can stop doing this whenever I decide I'm thin enough!"

A poor diet may result in severe loss of energy.

Going Downhill

Lorna was stretched out on her bed. She was so tired that she could barely move. Haley looked at her. Lorna looked pale and sick. Her hair was falling out, and her skin was very dry.

"I think you are becoming anorexic," Haley told her friend. "And you are totally obsessed with exercising!"

"That's crazy," Lorna said in a weak voice. "You remember what Mrs. Bernard said about *anorexia nervosa*. I don't have that disease, Haley. I can stop fasting whenever I want!"

"Anorexia nervosa can lead to convulsions and heart failure! It can make your bones thin. It can lead to an early death!" Haley gave a deep sigh.

"I'm not going to stop fasting until the kids at school call me 'skinny'!" Lorna vowed. She dragged herself off the bed and began exercising.

After several months the girls at school finally mentioned that Lorna was "skinny." The boys noticed too. But that didn't matter. When guys tried to talk to Lorna she really didn't care. She was depressed all the time. All she thought about was food that she couldn't eat!

One day Lorna fainted at school. As she rested on a cot in the nurse's office, Mrs. Bernard talked with her.

"You've been starving your body of the nutrients you need," she said gently. "That is dangerous, Lorna. You can't continue this way."

"I'll be okay," Lorna insisted. "I'll start eating more when I feel better."

"Your pulse rate is very low, and you said you are always cold. Those are symptoms of anorexia nervosa," Mrs. Bernard continued. "I think you and your parents should see a doctor. You have a psychological problem that is destroying your health."

Lorna knew Mrs. Bernard was right. She was tired of always feeling sick. She wanted to stop fasting, but she couldn't.

Getting Help

"I'll talk to your mom about getting you help," Mrs. Bernard went on. "You need to learn why you are injuring your body by fasting. Young women your age especially need to eat foods rich in calcium and iron. If they don't eat properly they often have bone problems later in life."

Lorna explained how Haley was losing weight. She asked if Haley should go to the doctor, too. Mrs. Bernard said she would talk to Haley that day.

"I'm proud of you both!" Mrs. Bernard told Lorna and Haley at the end of the term. Both girls were eating a variety of low-calorie foods. They were eating small portions, and they had kept their weight at a normal level.

"You've done a good job of turning your lives around," Mrs. Bernard continued. "You've learned that there is more to dieting than starving yourself. Now you make responsible choices for your diet!"

UNDERWEIGHT

Burt was one of the shortest guys in ninth grade, and very underdeveloped. In high school, his life became miserable.

"I've got to drop physical education!" he told his father one evening. "I come in last in every race. I'm always picked last for every team."

"You'll catch up with the other guys," Burt's father replied. "When your body starts maturing, you may even be taller than many of them."

"It's not just my height, Dad. I'm failing P.E. I just stand around on the side lines."

Burt's father lowered his newspaper and said, "I know a way to handle this. Professional athletes train before each season. They get fit so they can play better. They don't play to get fit."

Walking and exercising whenever possible can help to increase appetite and improve fitness.

"So how does that help me, Dad?"

"We both need to get physically fit. I need to lose some flabbiness, and you need to strengthen and build your muscles. Then you'll play sports better."

"How would we do that?" Burt was puzzled.

"Regular exercise is the answer. A better diet will give us the energy we'll need."

A Team Effort

That evening, Burt and his father walked over to the library. They took out books on physical fitness and diet. Burt was tired when they got home, but he was excited about their project.

"Call the 'Y' tomorrow," his mother suggested. "I know they offer swim classes. Swimming should improve the skills you need for group sports!"

Burt began walking to and from school. He also took swimming lessons. To his surprise, he enjoyed being out in the fresh air. And he really loved swimming!

Burt didn't get physically fit overnight. But in several months his muscles began to feel firmer. He had more energy, and he felt better about himself.

By the end of the term Burt noticed a difference during P.E. class. He ran up and down the basketball court without getting out of breath. He wasn't the last one to finish running around the track. And much to his relief, he wasn't the last one picked for team sports anymore.

"COUCH POTATO"

Reggie was 13. He loved to watch TV and eat junk food. Sitting down playing video games was even more fun.

Reggie was overweight, but he didn't care. His friends called him a "couch potato" because he never played outside with them. That didn't bother Reggie either. He hated to exercise.

Reggie went to the doctor for a physical checkup. He knew his doctor would tell him to lose weight. That didn't worry him. But Reggie's thumbs hurt from playing too many video games and that did worry him.

"You are exercising your thumbs too much and your body too little!" the doctor warned. "Your cholesterol is way too high. I've told you for years that you *should* lose weight. Now I'm telling you that you *must* lose weight!"

"What does high cholesterol do?" Reggie asked.

"High cholesterol injures your blood vessels. Fat is deposited in your veins and clogs them up. Then blood cannot flow to your heart as easily. That often leads to heart problems."

Reggie sighed. "So I can't eat butter and stuff like that?"

"Right. Butter is a saturated fat. You must eat fewer saturated fats, and less meat. Drink skim milk or low-fat milk instead of whole milk."

"I can handle that," Reggie agreed.

"You also must avoid chocolate, nuts, ice cream, and dairy products made with whole milk. They all have too much saturated fat," the doctor explained.

"Remember, fried foods absorb some of the oil in which they are fried. That adds fat even to healthful foods like chicken and fish."

Reggie made a face and groaned.

"You need to read food labels very carefully to check for fats. Coconut oil and palm oil are high in saturated fat even though they are vegetable fats. Try to avoid them."

"Is that all?" Reggie's head was spinning. His life was going to be ruined! How could he live without chocolate?

"You *must* exercise. When you get your cholesterol lower, you can eat small amounts of the foods you miss, Reggie. The trick is not to 'pig out' on them!"

—

Too much sitting and snacking may cause a variety of health problems.

Getting the Word

"What happens if I don't do all this stuff?" Reggie asked.

"You will have health problems sooner or later," the doctor answered.

Reggie was quiet as he thought about what the doctor had told him. Finally he asked, "Would riding my bike help?"

"It should. Ride for at least 30 minutes 3 times a week, and we'll take another blood test next month. If you stick to low-fat foods and ride your bike, that might be enough!"

"Are you going to tell my mom?"

"I'm going to call her in and we will discuss this together. She can help you with your meals at home. But lunch at school is totally your responsibility, Reggie. No one can do this for you!"

"I know," Reggie admitted.

For the next month, Reggie ate mostly low-fat foods. He rode his bike for 30 minutes every day after he got home from school. He found that he didn't miss watching TV as much as he thought he would. He met new kids in the neighborhood who also rode their bikes. By the time he went for his one-month checkup, he was riding every day for nearly an hour.

"You're doing great!" the doctor told him when he read Reggie's blood report. "Your cholesterol level has come down quite a bit. Stick with the diet and the exercise."

SEXUAL HYGIENE

Blair was almost 16. She was pretty but not very smart. She hated to brush her teeth. So she chewed a lot of gum to cover up her bad breath. She took two-minute showers that hardly got her wet and certainly didn't get her clean. So she used lots of perfume.

"Blair, you look like something the cat dragged in!" her mother often yelled at her. "When are you going to grow up and take responsibility for the way you look?"

"I took a shower yesterday in P.E.," Blair would tell her mother. Then she would tune her mother out. She couldn't be bothered with details like personal hygiene. Blair had her own ideas about things. She thought she had all the answers.

"Unsafe" Sex

Soon after Blair became 16 she met Zach. She fell in love. And she began to take better care of herself. Blair and Zach planned to marry after they had graduated from high school and found jobs.

Blair and Zach dated every evening. They saw so much of each other that their relationship got out of hand. One evening they decided not to wait to have sex.

"I don't have any condoms with me," Zach said. "But you know I don't do drugs. And I don't have HIV or AIDS!"

"Condoms aren't 100 percent safe anyway," Blair replied. "It's our first time having sex. Nothing will happen."

But something did happen. Once was enough for Blair to become pregnant. All of her crying didn't change that.

Blair knew she had been careless. Now she knew that she must take responsibility for herself and her baby. "I'm sorry, Mom," she said through her tears. "I'll do whatever it takes to be a good mother to my baby."

Blair and her mother made an appointment to see a doctor. Blair told him, "I want to learn to eat right. I want my baby to be healthy."

"That's a smart choice," the doctor said. "Your baby depends on you to grow and develop normally. A balanced diet will help both of you!"

Part of staying healthy is being responsible about sex.

CHAPTER

8

SUMMARY

You are likely to live longer and better if you stay fit and trim. Exercise helps you stay fit. Healthful food choices help you stay trim. Mental exercise helps you feel good.

You must know what you eat if you want to make smart food choices. Check food labels carefully. Many labels list calories, cholesterol, fats, and fiber.

Sometimes chemicals called preservatives are added to foods to help keep them from spoiling. Other additives may be added to make the food look or taste better. Some people are allergic to some additives.

A healthful diet includes foods from the five basic food groups. Vegetables, fruits, milk and yogurt,

Between-meal snacks can be healthy and can add to your daily
nutritional requirements.

meat, poultry, fish, bread, cereals, grains, and fats all help meet your nutritional needs. Also, drink plenty of water.

Exercise will help you stay healthy. Walking is easy, cheap, and good for you. Walk instead of ride whenever you can.

Don't be too hard on yourself if you slip up now and then. You may need time to develop good diet and exercise habits that make for a healthy life-style.

You owe it to yourself to stay as healthy as possible. And only you can do that.

Where to Go for Help

School nurses, doctors, dentists, or other health-care professionals can offer you information and help with various health problems.

DIAL-A-DIETITIAN
The American Dietetic Association's Nutrition Information Hotline:
1-800-366-1655 (Call 10 A.M.-5 P.M. Eastern Standard Time to talk with a registered dietitian. Call 24 hours a day for recorded information).

The TEEN/TAP (Teen Teaching AIDS Prevention) Call toll-free: 1-800-234-TEEN

BASH (Bulimia-Anorexia Self-Help) Call toll-free: 1-800-762-3334 or 1-800-227-4785

Public Health Service, Center for Disease Control Hotline: 1-800-442-0366

GLOSSARY
EXPLAINING NEW WORDS

amino acid One of a number of nutrients from which proteins are made that are necessary to a healthful diet.

anorexia nervosa Eating disorder characterized by fear of becoming fat and by excessive dieting.

bulimia Eating disorder characterized by excessive eating followed immediately by vomiting.

calcium Mineral that is needed for building strong bones and teeth.

carbohydrate Nutrient that is a source of energy for the body. Sugar and starch are carbohydrates.

condom Thin sheath, usually of rubber, worn on the penis during sexual intercourse to prevent conception or infection by disease.

dental floss String-like material that removes food and plaque stuck between teeth.

immune system Body's mechanism to prevent disease.

iron Mineral that is used to make red blood cells.

nutrients Parts of food that are needed by your body for growth, to repair body cells, and for energy.

plaque Sticky material that forms on the teeth. It can be prevented by brushing regularly.

protein Nutrient that is used by your body for growth and repair.

vitamin Nutrient that helps your body use proteins, carbohydrates, and fats.

FOR FURTHER READING

Bershad, Carol, and Bernick, Deborah. *Bodyworks.* New York: Random House, 1979.

Burns, Sheila L. *Allergies and You.* New York: Julian Messner, 1980.

Fretz, Sada. *Going Vegetarian: A Guide for Teenagers.* New York: Morrow, 1983.

Goodbody, Slim. *The Healthy Habits Handbook.* New York: Coward-McCann, 1983.

Hyman, Jane, M.Ed., and Posner, Barbara Millen, D.P.H., R.D. *The Fitness Book.* New York: Julian Messner, 1984.

Lukes, Bonnie L. *How to Be a Reasonably Thin Teenage Girl.* New York: Atheneum, 1986.

Perl, Lila. *Junk Food, Fast Food, Health Food: What America Eats and Why.* Boston: Houghton-Mifflin, 1980.

Rourke, Arlene C. *Looking Good: Diet and Exercise.* Vero Beach, FL: Rourke Publications, 1987.

Simon, Nissa. *Don't Worry, You're Normal: A Teenager's Guide to Self-Help.* New York: Corwell, 1982.

Ward, Brian R. *Dental Care.* New York: Franklin Watts, 1986.

————. *The Environment and Health.* New York: Franklin Watts, 1989.

Zizmor, Jonathan, and English, Diane. *Doctor Zizmor's Guide to Clearer Skin.* New York: Lippincott, 1980.

INDEX

About the Authors
   Jane Hurwitz holds an MA in Economics from the University of Kansas. She is coauthor of *Sally Ride: Shooting for the Stars*. In addition to writing for young adults, she has worked as an economist.

   Sue Hurwitz holds an MA in Education from the University of Missouri. She has taught every grade, K-9. Sue is coauthor of *Drugs and Your Friends, Hallucinogens*, and *Drugs and Birth Defects*.

Photo Credits
All photos on cover and in book by Dru Nadler.

Design & Production by Blackbirch Graphics.